CHAMPIONS OF FREEDOM
Volume 11

THE INTERNATIONAL ECONOMIC ORDER

The Hillsdale College Press
Hillsdale, Michigan 49242

Hillsdale College Press

Books by George Roche; the *Champions of Freedom* series from the Ludwig von Mises Lecture Series on economic policy; *The Christian Vision: Man in Society; The Essential Imprimis* collection; the CCA–Shavano video and cassette tapes; and the easy-to-read, humorous *Alternatives* program materials to explain the economic facts of life, are all available from the HILLSDALE COLLEGE PRESS, directed by Peter McCarty.

CHAMPIONS OF FREEDOM:
THE INTERNATIONAL ECONOMIC ORDER
© 1985 by Hillsdale College Press
Hillsdale, Michigan 49242

Printed in the United States of America

First Printing 1985
Library of Congress Catalog Card Number: 83-641096
ISBN 0-916308-98-7

Ludwig von Mises, who died in 1973 at the age of 92, was one of our century's most prominent defenders of human liberty and a dedicated opponent of governmental intervention in the economy. Through his scholarship, writing, and teaching, von Mises argued powerfully for individual freedom, private property, free markets, and limited government. His theory of economics was based on the supremacy of the individual and the rational, purposeful day-to-day decisions of the individual that constitute the market. His description of the market as a process, set against a background of fluctuating conditions, was a decisive departure from other contemporary economists' "models" of mathematical rigidity. In nineteen books, including his famous *Human Action* and *The Theory of Money and Credit*, hundreds of articles, and countless lectures, Dr. von Mises successfully proved that a free society cannot exist without a free economy.

1955 photo courtesy of Bettina Bien Greaves of The Foundation for Economic Education, Inc.

However, he wrote his books at a time when the dominant thinking in economics was against him. On this subject, in his own words, he said:

> Occasionally, I entertained the hope that my writings would bear practical fruit and show the way for policy. Constantly I have been looking for evidence of a change in ideology. But I have never allowed myself to be deceived. I have come to realize that my theories explain the degeneration of a great civilization; they do not prevent it. I set out to be a reformer, but only became the historian of decline.

Perhaps Mises has become the historian of decline, but the end is not yet. When the history of twentieth-century thought is written, Ludwig von Mises will in all probability be recognized as the greatest economist of our age. This may be wishful thinking, but I think not. I believe the truth always triumphs. It is always recognized, if only, as the economist is so fond of saying, in the long run. Without a doubt, when socialism is dead, when Marx is finally laid to rest, and when Keynesian economics is finally fully discredited, still Mises will live on.

George C. Roche III
President
Hillsdale College

CONTENTS

Preface

Now in its eleventh year, Hillsdale College's Center for Constructive Alternatives (CCA) is pleased to present the five distinguished lecturers from the 1983-84 Ludwig von Mises Lecture Series. This series, an integral part of the College's commitment to continue the work begun by Ludwig von Mises, provides a forum for leading economists, policy makers, and individuals to treat major economic questions confronting our society with Misean economic principles. The Mises lecturers also play a valuable role in Hillsdale's undergraduate Misean department of economics.

Each year, the lecturers from this series are gathered together into a book, *Champions of Freedom*, and published by the Hillsdale College Press.

In addition to offering the yearly lecture series and using the works of Dr. von Mises in its economics courses, Hillsdale has established the Ludwig von Mises Chair in Economics. The College is also the repository of Mises' entire personal library of over 5,000 volumes. This special collection, housed in the Ludwig von Mises Room of the college library, is used frequently by students and visiting scholars alike.

Special thanks go to Professors Charles Van Eaton (chairman), James Edwards, and Richard Grant of the Hillsdale College department of economics; Pat Dubois, CCA administrative assistant; and Nancy Steward, secretary in the public affairs office.

Peter C. McCarty, Director
Center for Constructive Alternatives

Lynne Morris, Senior Editor
Hillsdale College Press

Foreword

In 1983-84, for the first time in the history of the Ludwig von Mises Lecture Series, all the lecturers addressed a single theme: The International Monetary System, Its Nature, Operation and Reform. In keeping with this theme the first lecturer, Dr. David Laidler of the University of Western Ontario, discussed the meaning and implications of the monetary explanation of balance of payments and exchange rate phenomena.

It is clearly appropriate that Dr. Laidler's topic should open the 1983-84 von Mises lecture series. Virtually all the elements of the modern monetary theory of the balance of payments are elaborated in the original 1912 German edition of von Mises' *The Theory of Money and Credit*. The fresh insights which Dr. Laidler's paper brings to this topic make an important contribution to current debate on this important theme.

Our second lecturer, Dr. Leland Yeager of the University of Virginia, addressed issues relating to what is called "a commodity reserve currency." Under such a system all money — both in the U.S. as well as in other major trading nations — would be tied, by way of convertibility, to a bundle of traded commodities including gold, wheat, and other such basic raw materials. This idea, which had earlier been discussed by F. A. Hayek, is, despite its complexity, gaining increased attention in scholarly, if not yet in political, circles.

The third lecture by Professor Melvyn Krauss of New York University posed the question, "Is Reagan Losing the Battle of Ideas in the Third World?" Professor Krauss' point is that the U.S. should, as a matter of deliberate policy, proclaim to the economically less-developed nations of the world that their economic interests are best served by free markets and free trade. It was Professor Krauss' contention that we have not been pursuing this objective.

The fourth lecture, by Professor Kurt Leube of the Hoover Institution, was a development of F. A. Hayek's work on the "Denationalization of Money." Since Leube once served as Hayek's close research assistant, he was thoroughly familiar with this argument for wresting monopoly control over the supply of money from government and allowing both the supply of money and its exchange value to be determined by the free market.

What these first four speakers all have in common is that they are each professionally trained economists and academicians. They addressed the topics assigned to them — topics relating to international trade, finance and money — from a purely, and some might say "other worldly," perspective.

The fifth speaker, Mr. Anthony Harrigan, is, unlike the first four lecturers, neither an economist nor an academician. He is a businessman and a journalist who currently serves as Executive Director of a trade association. His topic was "International Trade Policy: Is There Such a Thing?"

Mr. Harrigan's topic expressed ideas first presented in an article he wrote for *National Review* in April, 1983, entitled "Needed: A Strategic Economic Policy." In that article, he argued that the usual academic argument for free trade under any and all circumstances is incorrect. We now need, he argued, some sort of system of protectionism in the form of tariffs and/or quotas until our own manufacturing industries can get on a sound footing which will allow them to compete in today's dynamic world economy.

Clearly the arguments expressed by Mr. Harrigan are in opposition to the free-trade views espoused by Ludwig von Mises, in whose honor these lectures are held. Some might wonder about the appropriateness of entertaining such a view in this setting. Yet rather than express concern, the case can be made that Mr. Harrigan's views should be seen within the context of von Mises' well-known love for the free flow of ideas in the open market of opinion.

Mr. Harrigan's contribution and the setting in which they are presented are certainly consistent with the principles which guided the scholarly work of Ludwig von Mises.

Dr. Charles D. Van Eaton
Hillsdale College
March 15, 1985

Contributors

David Laidler

A native of the United Kingdom, but now a Canadian citizen, David Laidler earned his B.S. in economics, with first-class honors, at the London School of Economics. He pursued graduate work at Syracuse University, earning a master's degree, and at the University of Chicago where he obtained his Ph.D. in economics. Since 1975, Professor Laidler has taught at the University of Western Ontario. He has also been a visiting professor at Brown University, the Stockholm School of Economics, the University of Konstanz, and Monash University. He served as general editor of the Manchester University Press Inflation Series and is an associate editor of the *Journal of Money, Credit and Banking*. Dr. Laidler is the author of four books, among them *The Demand for Money — Theories and Evidence* and *Monetarist Perspectives*, the editor of three others, and a frequent contributor to many professional publications.

Leland Yeager

Since 1969, Leland Yeager has served as the Paul Goodloe McIntire Professor in the department of economics at the University of Virginia. Previous to that, he taught at the University of Maryland and as a visiting professor at Texas A&M, Southern Methodist, UCLA, NYU, and Auburn. Dr. Yeager is an adjunct scholar of the American Enterprise Institute and the Cato Institute as well as a member of various advisory boards. He is the author of *Free Trade: America's Opportunity, International Monetary Relations: Theory, The International Monetary Mechanism*, among others, and numerous articles. Dr. Yeager is a Phi Beta Kappa graduate of Oberlin College and earned his M.A. and Ph.D. from Columbia University.

Melvyn Krauss

Melvyn Krauss is a professor of economics at New York University, a position he has held since 1976. He is also a senior fellow at the Hoover Institution of Stanford University. Visiting professorships have taken him all over the world, to the Universities of Mannheim, Western Ontario, Columbia, Aix-Marseilles II, Stockholm, Stanford, and the London School of Economics. In addition, he has taught at Johns Hopkins and the Europa Institut of the University of Amsterdam. He specialized in economics at every academic level, earning a B.A. from Brooklyn College and his M.A. and Ph.D. at New York University. Dr. Krauss is the author of *Development Without Aid, The New Protectionism, A Geometric Approach to International Trade*, and *General Equilibrium Analysis* as well as over fifty articles dealing with economics.

Kurt Leube

Kurt Leube, an expert in fundamental questions of political economy, economic philosophy and ideology, is presently with the Hoover Institution of Stanford University. He was born in Salzburg, Austria, and was educated at the Universities of Vienna, Innsbruck, Freiburg, and Salzburg, earning his J.D. in economics in 1971. From 1969 to 1977, Dr. Leube was a research assistant to and associate of F. A. von Hayek at the University of Salzburg. From 1977 until recently, he held an academic position with the Association of Austrian Industrialists. Dr. Leube is editor-in-chief of both *The International Carl Menger Library* and *Prokontra. Zur Politischen Oekonomie* book series. He is also the author of dozens of articles and translations, and holds membership in a number of international societies.

Anthony Harrigan

Anthony Harrigan is currently president of both the United States Industrial Council and the United States Industrial Council Educational Foundation. His previous work as an editorial writer and reporter took him to many parts of Latin America, Africa, and the Far East. A prolific writer, he is the author, co-author, and editor of eight books published in the U.S. and abroad between 1954 and 1976, and a contributor to more than 34 journals. He is also a guest lecturer at a number of colleges across the country. Mr. Harrigan continues to write a newspaper column published in over 150 daily papers. He was educated at Bard College, Kenyon College, and the University of Virginia.

David Laidler

The "Monetary Approach" and the International Monetary System

I. The Monetary Approach

There are two ways of defining the so-called "monetary approach" to balance-of-payments and exchange-rate analysis. It may be characterized as a theoretical framework which enables one to organize arguments about international monetary matters in a particular way, or as a specific set of hypotheses about the causes of balance-of-payments flows and exchange-rate changes.

As a theoretical framework, the approach is easily described. It tells us that discussions of balance-of-payments and exchange-rate matters may be organized around the interaction of the supply and demand for money. An economy in which the domestic credit creation activities of the banking system are tending to cause the money supply to grow faster than the demand for money will, under a fixed exchange rate,

1

find itself losing foreign exchange reserves, and, under a flexible rate, will tend to face a depreciating currency; and vice versa.

The monetary approach thus characterized provides a particular way of looking at things, but it does not, in and of itself, lead to predictions which differ from those of other, more traditional approaches to the same problem area, provided that these are applied correctly. It should not matter, when we study the international monetary relations of a particular country, whether we look at the factors affecting trade flows and capital flows, and then derive from the results obtained in this way conclusions about what must happen on the monetary front, or whether we start instead with the supply and demand for money: we should get to the same place in one way or the other, and there is no reason why one particular route should always be easier.

As a theoretical matter, it is quite possible that most sources of balance-of-payments or exchange-rate disturbance lie on the real side of the economy, in changes in tastes and technology, in shifts in saving propensities and the productivity of investment. It is possible to deduce the consequences of changes such as these for the demand for money and then to use the monetary approach to draw conclusions about their effects on the balance of payments and the exchange rate, but such a procedure may often be clumsy. The monetary approach, for obvious reasons, is best suited to dealing with situations in which the major source of exchange-rate and balance-of-payments disturbance lies in fluctuations on the supply side of the monetary system. That is why it is often thought of as encompassing a particular set of empirical hypotheses as well.

To many people, integral to the monetary approach are the hypothesis of a stable aggregate demand for money function and the proposition that the dominant impulse driving international monetary disturbances is fluctuations in the credit-creating activities of the banking system, potentially in response to private-sector borrowing, but usually as a result of monetizing government deficits. It is no accident that these two concrete propositions about how the world in fact works derive from the work of Milton Friedman (e.g., 1956) and Karl Brunner and Allan Meltzer (e.g., 1978), because, as a substantive body of theory, the monetary approach is in fact an adaptation of closed-economy "monetarism" to international questions.

Now, the monetary approach is not a new product of the last twenty years or so. Much more than its outlines can be discerned in the writings of Richard Cantillon (1755) and of course in those of David Hume (1752); a form of it lies at the heart of the British monetary debates of the Revolutionary and Napoleonic Wars. The Austrian economists, not least von Mises himself, employed a version of the doctrine. The work of Harry Johnson (1972) and Robert Mundell (1971) certainly had new things to say about how prices are determined in world markets, about the precise transmission mechanisms linking monetary disturbances to balance-of-payments and exchange-rate changes, and inspired much econometric work of a type not seen earlier. Nevertheless, this modern work contributed to the refinement of a set of ideas which have a long and honorable history in liberal economic thought, though it did not create that set of ideas (nor did its authors claim that it had done so).

As Dr. James Edwards of Hillsdale College has pointed out to me, interest in one form or another of the monetary approach has waxed and waned over the years, and has usually been at its strongest during or just after periods of great monetary upheaval. That is not an accident, because such periods are precisely those in which fluctuations in real factors are swamped by those originating in the monetary system, and in which, therefore, the substantive hypotheses, mentioned above as forming an integral part of the modern monetary approach, are most in accord with empirical experience. As no one needs reminding, we are now living in a period of monetary instability, and that is no doubt why a version of the monetary approach is in style. I hope that its usefulness will be amply illustrated by the rest of this lecture.

II. The Bretton Woods System

No one possessing the least familiarity with the ideas of Austrian economics will be surprised to learn that the international system of monetary relationships known as the "Bretton Woods system" did not develop in practice as its founders had intended. The intention after the second world war was to put the world back on to a form of gold exchange standard, which would nevertheless permit exchange rates to be varied in an orderly and coordinated way when circumstances seemed to require it. Instead, the system evolved into a United States dollar standard, in which exchange rates were changed with much less frequency than the founders of the system had intended. Even so, if the object of the exercise was to provide a monetary system which would underpin the creation of a liberal international economic order, it was a success for close to two decades.

Although the U.S. dollar was convertible freely into gold at a fixed price of $35 per ounce (but not for American residents!), gold convertibility played no part in determining the conduct of U.S. monetary policy (see Darby, Lothian et al. [1983]). In the 1950s and early 1960s that policy was nevertheless remarkably stable. The U.S. dollar was essentially inflation free, and because the international economic system needed a readily acceptable money of reliable purchasing power to underpin it, the dollar naturally evolved as the reserve currency of an integrated international monetary system. In the 1950s and 1960s, therefore, the Federal Reserve system made monetary policy for the whole Western world.

Outside the United States, this entire period was the heyday of Keynesian economics. Governments such as that of the United Kingdom not only attempted to fine tune their aggregate economic performance, but succeeded in doing so. They were able to do this because they were also committed to maintaining a particular exchange rate on the U.S. dollar. When their monetary policies became too expansionary as a result of financing fiscal deficits, the effects fell not so much upon domestic prices but, as the monetary approach predicts, on the balance of payments: the "need" to maintain the exchange rate then provided an incentive to moderate the expansionary policies.

The Bretton Woods system provided price stability for the Western world, but it did so as a result of two preconditions whose role was only properly understood with the benefit of hindsight. First, the governments of individual countries had to be willing to continue to give priority to the maintenance of the exchange rate when to do so apparently conflicted with the pursuit of purely domestic goals; and second, and absolutely critically, the United States had to remain inflation free. The 1960s saw both of these preconditions undermined.

It was during the 1960s that the idea of a stable policy trade-off between inflation and unemployment became popular. Policymakers in some countries began to see the obligation to maintain a fixed exchange rate as an obstacle to achieving the full benefits of Keynesian policies. It seemed to them that they could, by generating a little more inflation accompanied by a continuous devaluation against the United States dollar, obtain a permanent gain in levels of employment. Of course the argument was nonsense, and was quickly exposed as such by those who recognized that it was based upon the fantastic assumption that economic agents are afflicted with perpetual money illusion and hence do not notice when inflation affects the purchasing power of their incomes (see Friedman [1968], Mundell [1971]). Nevertheless, it took close to a decade of bitter experience to convince the majority of what is often called "informed opinion" of this; and their alleged ability to enable policymakers to exploit the inflation–unemployment trade-off became a key part of the case for flexible exchange rates in the 1960s.

Even more crucially, in the 1960s the United States began to become inflation prone. From 1962 onward, "Keynesian" ideas began to inform her domestic policy, including the notion of an inflation–unemployment trade-off. At the same time, the war in Vietnam grew in scale, and the Johnson administration found it expedient, as wartime governments so often do, to turn to the printing press to finance its military expenditures. Historians will no doubt argue for many years to come about which of these forces contributed most to the onset of the United States's inflation in the 1960s, but from our point of view, it doesn't much matter.

The crucial point in the current context is that, because under the Bretton Woods system the United States was providing the reserve currency for the international monetary system, her balance of payments, unlike that of any other country, did not provide an automatic check on excessive domestic money creation. The basic mechanism to which the monetary approach points, in the shape of the link between domestic credit expansion and a balance-of-payments deficit, surely enough worked in the United States's case; but the deficit in its turn simply led to a step-up in the rate at which world liquidity grew, rather than to any reversal of domestic policy. Other countries began, on average, to experience balance-of-payments surpluses, whose effects on their domestic money supplies they could sterilize only for a short time. The inflation generated by United States monetary policy therefore occurred not just in the United States, but throughout the Bretton Woods system.

In short, in the 1960s for a variety of reasons, different countries began to take different views about what constituted desirable inflation rates and about the likely consequences of particular policies for inflation. Quite understandably (but not necessarily excusably), the pursuit of domestic ends came to dominate economic policies, and different national governments began to attach different degrees of priority to maintaining price-level stability.

When inflation becomes an object of political debate and choice, and when the highest level of effective political authority exists at the level of the nation state, a system of fixed exchange rates is not viable. The breakdown of the Bretton Woods system and the piecemeal adoption of flexible exchange rates in the 1970s simply reflected the monetary consequence of a basic fact of international political life, namely a growing tendency for the governments of nation states to design economic policies with a view to achieving purely national goals.

III. Experience with Flexible Exchange Rates

To say that flexible exchange rates are a natural accompaniment to economic policies aimed at achieving domestic ends does not mean that those of us who are concerned with promoting a liberal international economic order should oppose them. We might well wish that "Keynesian" thought had not come to dominate so much post-war discussion of economic policies toward employment and inflation, and that the political processes of different countries had not generated policy targets which were incompatible with the simultaneous maintenance of fixed-exchange rates and relatively free movement of goods and capital among countries. We might also have preferred it if the Bretton Woods system had in fact imposed sufficient anti-inflationary discipline on various governments so that these political processes had not resulted in the economic policies which were pursued in the 1960s.

However, macro-economic policies based on "Keynesian" ideas did become inconsistent among the countries of the Western world in the 1960s, and flexible exchange rates provided what might loosely be called a "second-best" solution to the problem of preserving a liberal international order in the face of this inconsistency. By the beginning of the 1970s the alternative to flexible exchange rates was not the maintenance of the Bretton Woods system and continued free movement of goods and capital. The monetary approach tells us quite clearly that, given the domestic fiscal and monetary policies which were then in place, this would have been impossible.

Had a determined attempt to maintain fixed rates been made in the 1970s, it would have had to involve widespread use of tariffs and quotas to control trade flows, and exchange controls to suppress capital movements. Thus, and as Milton Friedman (1953) had argued long before the event, in a world in which national governments were determined to go their own ways with domestic macro-economic policies, flexible exchange rates provided the only hope of preserving liberalism in the international economy.

Nevertheless, there can be no denying that flexible exchange rates in the 1970s did not function quite as their advocates had predicted. Exchange rates moved with much greater frequency and amplitude than anyone had expected, and instability in the international monetary system became, and remains, a major cause for concern. It is important to keep a sense of proportion here. The international monetary system has certainly been volatile in recent years, but it has not, in and of itself, been an important independent source of economic instability. Rather it has transmitted, and on some occasions amplified, the effects of instability arising elsewhere in the world economy. To blame flexible exchange rates for our recent troubles is like blaming the messenger for the quality of the news he has brought.

Let it be clear that, when I refer here to other sources of instability, I do not mean those factors most often pointed to in popular discussions: namely bad harvests, commodity price explosions, the behavior of OPEC, and so on. Bad harvests obviously are exogenous events and did not help matters in the 1970s, but the other phenomena which are so often cited as independent causes of international monetary instability were in fact consequences of the very same fundamental forces which created exchange-rate volatility. The monetary approach tells us to look for the sources of exchange-rate variations in the interaction of the supplies and demand for various national currencies, and postulates as an empirical matter that the dominant impulse driving disturbances will usually be found on the supply side of the market. This basic insight is amply borne out by the experience of the 1970s.

When the Bretton Woods system broke down, the international economy did not cease to exist. Trade in goods and capital continued to grow during the 1970s. International transactions still needed to be invoiced, international debts still had to be denominated in some monetary unit or another, bills still had to be paid across national boundaries using some currency as a means of exchange, and so on. Under Bretton Woods, the U.S. dollar played the role of international unit of account, means of exchange, and store of value, and as McKinnon (e.g., 1979) in particular has stressed, it continued to do so on a large scale throughout the 1970s.

Instability in United States monetary policy did not, therefore, cease to affect the international monetary system in the 1970s; it merely ceased to affect directly the domestic monetary systems of other countries, and United States monetary policy did in fact continue to be unstable throughout the decade. We must not put all the blame on the United States, for certain other countries too, not least Canada and the United Kingdom, did their bit to provide an unstable monetary environment; but the continuing international role of the dollar lent a particular significance for the international economy to United States monetary policy, even under a flexible exchange-rate regime.

The international monetary system and international commodity markets did not simply transmit to the world economy the effects of unstable United States monetary policy. Rather they amplified those effects. It is a commonplace of elementary economics that, when the supply function of some item shifts, its price must change to re-equilibrate supply and demand, and this is as true of a particular national money as of anything else. However, in the case of money, the relevant "price" which must change is its purchasing power over everything else, including commodities and foreign monies.

If every money price were equally flexible, all would be well and good, but the money prices of many manufactured goods, not to mention those of labor, though not absolutely rigid by any means, are nevertheless sticky. The effects of changes in the money supply therefore tend, in a "short run" that may last for a year or more, to be concentrated on the money prices of those items which are traded in markets where prices are flexible. Commodities and foreign currencies fall into this latter category so that their prices tend to "overshoot" their long-run values in the face of monetary disturbances, thus creating relative price changes in response to monetary disturbances, which in their turn distort the pattern of economic activity.

Even the behavior of the price of oil in the 1970s can be explained to some extent in these terms. OPEC sets the price of oil in U.S. dollars, and so one would expect that cartel to take careful account of U.S. monetary policy in designing its pricing policy. It is no accident that both large oil price increases, those of 1973 and 1979, took place in the wake of explosions in United States monetary growth. For other commodities, whose markets are not dominated by cartels, and for exchange rates, the case is even more clear-cut.

It is perhaps surprising that the liberal nature of the international economy lasted as well as it did during the 1970s. Trade in both goods and capital continued to grow throughout the decade, despite the volatility of exchange rates. However, the experience of the last two or three years, when a sharp tightening-up of United States monetary policy has reverberated through the international economy, suggests that we cannot take the continuation of these favorable trends for granted. Trade protectionism has been growing, and the ongoing international debt crisis bears witness to the fact that the success of the international financial system, in coping with the stresses of "recycling" OPEC surpluses through capital markets, was not quite as unqualified as it initially appeared to be.

Perhaps the adoption of flexible exchange rates in the early 1970s will, in retrospect, turn out merely to have prolonged for a little while the life of the liberal international economic order created under the Bretton Woods system, rather than to have protected it permanently from the strains put upon it by national fiscal and monetary policies designed solely with domestic goals in mind. If those policies in the 1980s follow the pattern of the 1960s and 1970s, more protectionism in trade policy and further erosion of confidence in international capital markets look all too likely. However there are grounds, albeit uncertain ones, for taking a more optimistic view of our future, as I shall argue in the next, and final, section of this essay.

IV. The Matter of Monetary Reform

Given the instability of the last decade, it is small wonder that the question of how to reform the international monetary system with a view to stabilizing it is much discussed these days. The insights which the monetary approach yields concerning the breakdown of Bretton Woods and our subsequent experience with floating exchange rates yield immediate implications for this issue. As I have already remarked, the key to understanding recent monetary history lies in the recognition that instability of the international monetary system has been a consequence of instability in the conduct of domestic monetary policies in a number of countries, but above all in the United States. Any scheme, therefore, which seeks to reform the international monetary system without simultaneously taking steps to restore responsible monetary policies to the countries of the Western world will fail. Just as wage-and-price-control programs attempt to treat the symptoms of inflation without getting at its causes, so proposals to stabilize exchange rates and to regulate the supply of international liquidity through some "New Bretton Woods" also concentrate on the visible effects of an economic disorder whose causes lie elsewhere.

The early 1980s have already provided one concrete example of the futility of such schemes in the shape of the European Monetary System. Its aim was to stabilize exchange rates among the currencies of member countries of the European Economic Community with, in the eyes of some of its supporters, the ultimate goal of promoting a common currency for the community. Though the system did provide a set of rules and institutional arrangements for pegging, and if necessary changing, exchange rates, and though it established, in the shape of the European Currency Unit, a new international reserve currency and unit of account, it involved no concrete devices to promote the coordination of fiscal and monetary policies among member nations. Its very existence was supposed to be enough to promote such coordination, but of course it was not, as the recent behavior of the French franc and the Italian lira bear witness.

The EMS did, and indeed does, leave open the possibility of individual countries altering their parities. However, it does not seem to be correct to argue, as do some advocates of a return for the Western world to fixed exchange rates perhaps backed by some kind of commodity convertibility, that a system which required a firm commitment never to alter an exchange rate would provide effective external discipline on domestic policies, discipline which looser arrangements like the EMS fail to impose.

The difficulty here is that politicians and bureaucrats by now understand the implications of the monetary approach just as well as do academic economists. Those of them who wish to avoid undertaking policies which carry with them a risk of inflation might well be willing to accept such external discipline, but they will do so precisely because they are in no need of it. Those of them who feel impelled to leave open for themselves the option of choosing inflationary policies might be in sore need of the discipline of a commodity standard, but they will refuse to join such a system for just that reason. Discipline in domestic policies, that is to say, must come before and not after the stabilization of exchange rates.

It is in this last proposition that I find some, far from compelling, grounds for optimism about the future of the international monetary system. Indiscipline in macro-economic policies has its roots deep in political processes. Bad economics has something to do with it — people did believe in a stable inflation-unemployment tradeoff, for example — but before bad economics, however sincerely believed, can affect policy, there have to be buyers for it in the political marketplace. After fifteen years of monetary instability, electorates throughout the West are far more averse to taking risks on inflation, and far better informed about the crucial role of monetary policy in generating inflation, than they were in the mid-1960s.

It is not as good domestic politics as it was to advocate inflationary policies which, as a side effect, might disrupt international monetary relations. This is true in Western Europe, as the outcome of recent elections in West Germany and Britain, not to mention the reversal of policy that has recently taken place in France, show, and it is also true in the United States. If this tendency represents a long-run change in the political climate, and reasonable people can certainly disagree about this matter, then the international monetary system in the 1980s will be much more stable than it was in the 1970s. Flexible exchange rates can, to be sure, amplify shocks in a significant way, and hence contribute to the instability of the international economy, but only if they are subjected to shocks in the first place. If, for purely domestic reasons, domestic monetary policies become more responsible, then the international monetary system will settle down, and exchange rates, though nominally flexible, will tend to stabilize.

As I have already noted, the international economy is an entity in and of itself, and requires an international money to function efficiently. Under Bretton Woods, the United States dollar played this role, and, despite its recent instability, has continued to play an important role under flexible rates. One source of exchange-rate instability during the last decade has been attempts on the part of agents in the international economy to move into one alternative or another to the U.S. dollar when confidence in it has been particularly low. The mark, the yen, and the Swiss franc have all been subject to pressures emanating from this source.

The key point here should be easily acceptable to anyone familiar with Austrian ideas: what functions as an international money cannot be arranged by international agreement among governments. Rather, it is the outcome of choices, made by a myriad of agencies involved in international transactions about which currency they will use to denominate their current transactions and their debts, and about which currency they will use as an international means of exchange. Some of these agencies will be central banks and government departments, but overwhelmingly they will be private firms and individuals engaged in international transactions.

Though it is possible for the international economy to function with multiple monies, and nowadays it does so with the mark, the yen, the Swiss franc and so on each playing a role, particularly in specific regions of the world, one money is more efficient than many. Left to themselves, market forces tend to work in that direction — as the spread of the gold standard in the 19th century bears witness. There is no reason why those market forces should not cause the still dominant international money, the U.S. dollar, to reassume its role as the key currency of the international monetary system, provided that United States monetary policy is stabilized in the 1980s; nor if other countries also pursue stable monetary policies, is there any reason why the resulting stable exchange-rate structure should not then in due course be pegged by international agreement. If this does happen, then something like a "new Bretton Woods system" will have emerged. It will be the end product of a set of policies based upon a domestic political consensus in each country, and of the freely made choices of agents operating in the international economy. It will therefore be firmly based.

That is how things might work out in the 1980s and 1990s, and if they do, the recent erosion of liberalism in the international economy will be short-lived. One can only hope that this optimistic view of the future is borne out by experience; but one cannot, as I have already noted, take this for granted. In particular, none of these things will come to pass unless United States monetary policy regains the stability that characterized it in the 1950s and early 1960s. There currently exists one very large obstacle to this: I refer to the chronic imbalance of the federal government's budget.

I simply do not see how deficits in the $200 billion range can be sustained year by year without the U.S. government eventually being tempted to monetize them; and if it does succumb to that temptation, then the inflation which will follow will wreak havoc not only with the United States's domestic economy, but with the international economy as well. The best thing that the United States can do for the world economy, that is to say, is also the best thing that she can do for herself: namely put her fiscal house in order so that long-term monetary stability can be restored domestically, and hence to the rest of the world. Only then will the long-term future of a liberal international economic order be ensured.

REFERENCES

Brunner, K., and Meltzer, A. H., eds. *The Problem of Inflation: Carnegie-Rochester Conference Series on Public Policy.* Vol. 8. Amsterdam: North-Holland, 1978.

Cantillon, R. *Essai sur la nature du commerce en général.* Paris, 1755.

Darby, M., Lothian, J., et al. *The International Transmission of Inflation.* Chicago: University of Chicago Press for the NBER, 1983.

Friedman, M. "The Case for Flexible Exchange Rates," in *Essays in Positive Economics.* Chicago: University of Chicago Press, 1953.

Friedman, M. "The Quantity Theory of Money — A Restatement," in *Studies in the Quantity Theory of Money.* Chicago: University of Chicago Press, 1956.

Friedman, M. "The Role of Monetary Policy," *American Economic Review* 58 (March, 1968): 1–17.

Hume, D. *Essays, Moral, Political and Literary.* London, 1752.

Johnson, H. G. "The Monetary Approach to Balance of Payments Theory," in *Further Essays in Monetary Economics.* London: Allen and Unwin, 1972.

McKinnon, R. *Money in International Exchange.* London: Oxford University Press, 1979.

Mundell, R. *Monetary Theory.* Pacific Palisades: Goodyear, 1971.

Leland B. Yeager

America and a
Healthy World Monetary Order

The Bretton Woods system of fixed-exchange rates broke down for the last time in March 1973, and exchange rates began generally floating. Since then, the world has experienced wide fluctuations in bilateral rates. Changes have reached 10 and 20 percent over periods of months, 40 percent over a year or so, and sometimes several percents from day to day or even within days. As the asset-market theory of exchange rates helps us to understand, differences between national inflation rates and changing expectations about differences in the future become exaggerated in exchange-rate movements. Interest-rate differentials, and expectations about them, also play a prominent role.

When we say that the international monetary system has been working poorly in that respect and when we want to compare it with alternatives, we should be clear about what the system *is*. It is *not* the substantially free-floating system advocated by many academic economists since the 1950s and 1960s. Much rate-pegging and rate-management is still going on. At mid-1983 the currencies of 54 countries belonging to the International Monetary Fund were pegged to a single currency (most of them to the dollar), 14 currencies were pegged to the IMF's Special Drawing Right, and 25 were pegged to some other composite of currencies. Seventeen currencies were classified as having limited flexibility. These included the currencies of the eight members of the European Monetary System, which is a miniature Bretton Woods arrangement. Thirty-five currencies were classified as "more flexible." Only eight were floating independently.[1]

No such classification can be clear-cut. The significance of declared parities is undermined by their frequent adjustment or by wide margins of fluctuation around them. Both within and outside the European Monetary System, opportunities for one-way-option speculation on changes in pegged rates, so familiar under the Bretton Woods system, still recur. Currencies officially floating are often loosely pegged through large gains or losses of official reserves. Drawings on the International Monetary Fund to finance official interventions have grown since floating began; and the Fund has prepared for expanded operations by enlarging members' quotas, issuing new SDRs, and instituting new "facilities" for drawings. "Swap" lines of credit between the United States and other countries have expanded.

It is easy, with hindsight, to criticize "overtracking" or "overshooting" on the foreign-exchange market. It is less clear that the markets have been mistakenly processing the information actually available at the time. It is also an unsettled issue, in my judgment, whether official intervention,

changing in intensity and direction and character from time
to time, along with rumors about these changes, has made the
markets more or less jumpy, on the whole, than they would
have been in the known and dependable absence of intervention. (There is a pervasive tacit idea, which seems to be
dying harder in its application to foreign-exchange markets
than to other human affairs, that if some aspect of reality is
seen as unsatisfactory, government intervention is of course
the remedy. The unsatisfactoriness counts as argument
enough. But good intentions do not guarantee good results.)

To understand the nature of the current international
monetary system, it is useful to recall how it came onto the
scene. Forgetfulness and error on this question frequently
intertwine with recommendations for restoring the Bretton
Woods system. According to Alan Reynolds,[2] for example,
that fixed-rate system did not break down but was deliberately
destroyed. The truth is almost the reverse. Bretton Woods
never was intellectually abandoned. Policymakers in the
United States and abroad made repeated attempts to defend
that inherently flawed system and to repair it after it first
crumbled. They heralded the short-lived Smithsonian Agreement of December 1971 as a sound reconstruction of fixed-
exchange rates after their supposedly only temporary inter-
ruption. As Thomas de Vries of the International Monetary
Fund has candidly written, policymakers stuck to the old par-
value system with "almost unbelievable tenacity. . . . it took
three speculative waves of unimaginable proportions . . . to
move the world in March 1973 toward a more flexible
exchange-rate regime for an 'interim period,' after which par
values were to be gradually reestablished. . . . " The new system came into existence "as a result of breakdown" of the old.

The IMF's "Committee of Twenty . . . chose to ignore" this change and continued working for a system of "stable but adjustable par values."[3]

The current system of floating is thus emphatically not the result of policymakers' heeding the recommendations of academic economists.

During the last-ditch defense of the Bretton Woods system, foreign central banks bought up dollars to keep their own currencies from appreciating against the dollar beyond the prescribed limits. In so doing, they expanded their domestic monetary bases. The resulting worldwide explosion of national money supplies was followed by the worldwide surge of inflation in 1973–74.

It is a widespread fallacy to blame the speedup of inflation in the 1970s on floating exchange rates. Not even the *post hoc* premise of that fallacy is valid, since inflation began speeding up even before exchange rates began generally floating.

This speedup also preceded, and by several additional months, the Arab oil embargo and the quadrupling of oil prices in 1973–74. I do not mean to understate the contribution that this event made to inflation (like events affecting wheat, soybeans, and anchovies also). It is an all-too-familiar error, however, to focus on newsworthy events to the neglect of the less spectacular fundamentals. Even the emboldening of OPEC in the early 1970s seems itself to have been partly due to a U.S. State Department theory favoring the financial strengthening of anticommunist regimes in the Middle East and then to Western flabbiness in the face of unilateral modification of existing concession agreements by some oil countries. Further stimulus to OPEC action came from the boom around 1972 in wholesale commodity prices (which tend to respond sensitively and early to underlying inflation). OPEC could observe the loss of both purchasing power and foreign-exchange value by the dollar, in which it prices its oil. OPEC predation, in short, far from being the main cause, was partly a consequence of world inflation, itself largely due to unduly prolonged defense of the Bretton Woods system.

The transition to fluctuating exchange rates, far from being a result of rational deliberation, came about belatedly in almost the worst conceivable way. Those economists and policymakers who, back in the 1960s, when calm choice was still possible, argued for the status quo and patchwork measures on the grounds that a transition to fluctuating exchanges would be painful have proved wrong in a most ironic way.

I, for one, therefore, do not look for salvation through restoration of anything like the Bretton Woods system. The unsatisfactory behavior of exchange rates nowadays and the unsatisfactory state of international monetary relations in general cannot be remedied by governmental fiddling with the rates or by institutional gimmickry on the international scene. The trouble lies fundamentally with the national currencies that trade against one another on the foreign-exchange market.

Existing national monetary systems are preposterous in making each national unit of account (pricing unit, accounting unit) the supply-and-demand determined purchasing power of the unit in which the fiat medium of exchange is denominated. I lack space to explain fully, but I do judge that these domestic systems are the chief source of instability and disorder in exchange rates, price levels, production, employment, and economic calculation. Here is where reform must be sought.

I am not content with merely recommending "the" or "a" gold standard. Many types of gold standard have been either experienced historically or recommended. Some would amount to continuations of government-dominated fiat money with a role for gold grafted on as little more than a public-relations device. I join Milton Friedman[4] in warning against a mere pseudo gold standard.

I would gladly see the classical gold standard of the few decades before 1914 restored, if only we could undo the disasters that destroyed it, including World War I and all its consequences. Some institutions, though, once destroyed, just cannot be restored as they were; the preconditions, perhaps including ideologies or myths, cannot be constructed at will. F. A. Hayek has made this observation about the gold standard.[5]

More cheerful circumstances also argue against trying to bring back the gold standard of the past. Advances in economic theory and in technology (including marvels of communications and data processing), as well as many new institutions and practices introduced or made possible by financial innovators, have widened the range of free-enterprise-oriented monetary systems (and perhaps moneyless payments systems) among which we may ultimately choose.

Some libertarians and Austrian economists deplore deliberately trying to devise, assess, and choose among possible monetary systems of the future. "Let the market decide," they say. That is a cop-out. Our existing system, far from being the product of beneficent spontaneous evolution, has been haphazardly shaped over the decades and centuries by numerous piecemeal government interventions. Shifting to a more private or market-oriented system — or even just clearing the way for spontaneous evolution, if that is what we want — will require dismantling the government's current domination over money. The particular manner in which this dismantling takes place is bound to influence what type of new system will emerge. The government's major role in the economy, regrettable as it may be — its activities in taxation, spending, expressing the values of incomes and assets and debts, and accounting — is bound to influence what specific new system takes hold, and how readily. Furthermore, a certain inertia operates in the use of money as of language: Individuals have good reason to keep on using the one their fellows use, even though a different one might be preferable for the aggregate of individuals if they could all act together in choosing it.

If monetary evolution is to flow in more satisfactory channels, then, the government is bound to exert at least a nudge on that course, if only by the specific manner in which it gets out of the way. Rather than ignore that necessity, we should openly analyze and discuss what new system we would like the unavoidable nudge to favor.

Robert Greenfield and I have described a reform that would almost completely depoliticize money and banking.[6] The government would exert a noncoercive nudge toward replacing the dollar with a new unit of account. It would define the new unit in terms of a bundle of goods and services so comprehensive that its value would remain nearly stable against goods and services in general. The government would be barred from issuing money. Private enterprise, probably in the form of institutions combining the features of today's banks, money-market mutual funds, and stock mutual funds, would offer convenient media of exchange. Separating the unit of account from the medium — or rather media — of exchange, whose quantity would be appropriately determined largely by the demand for them, would go far toward avoiding both inflation and recession and facilitating stable prosperity.

The proposed system would lack money as we know it. People would probably make payments by writing checks, denominated in the defined unit of account, on their holdings of shares of stock in institutions combining the features of mutual funds and banks. (These shares would have market-determined flexible prices.) These practices would not entail the textbook inconveniences of barter. The advantages of having a single definite unit of account and convenient methods of payment would be retained and enhanced. The absurdities of linking the unit of account and medium of exchange in the present manner would be overcome.

Monetarism, to succeed, requires accurate adjustment of the quantity of money to the quantity demanded. It must therefore be suspicious of innovations that alter the supply–demand relation and even blur the concept of money. In sharp contrast, the system proposed here can positively welcome financial deregulation. The government can take just as much a laissez-faire stance toward the financial system, once it has offered and promoted a particular definition of the unit of account, as it can take toward ordinary businesses that happen to employ defined units of length and weight in their operations.

The proposed system may be too far out to stand a politically realistic chance of early adoption. Furthermore, I worry about problems of transition away from government money to purely private media of exchange. (In particular, if availability of new attractive alternatives punctures the demand for and value of government money, its existing holders will be expropriated unless the government replaces their holdings with bona fide interest-bearing government securities.)

These reasons recommend considering a second-best or fall-back reform that would stabilize government money rather than abolish it. A price-index rule might be combined with gold redeemability in a manner reminiscent of the "compensated dollar" proposed by Irving Fisher.[7] The Federal Reserve would be instructed to target its open-market operations on stabilizing a broad price index. It would also be required to redeem its money on demand in the quantity of gold — the changeable physical quantity — actually worth, at current prices, the bundle of goods and services used in specifying the price index. (The Federal Reserve would probably also be required to issue new money in exchange for the calculated amounts of gold, with a slight spread between its selling and buying prices of gold to cover expenses.)

Convertibility of this sort would be more than just decorative. It would impose an additional discipline on the monetary authority by requiring it actually to *do something* at the initiative of moneyholders. This discipline would work against overissue of money. Yet the value of money would not be exposed to the vagaries of the gold market. There could be no self-aggravating and destructive scramble for gold such as can occur under an ordinary fractional-reserve gold standard. Any scramble for gold would reflect itself in an increased money price and relative price of gold, automatically reducing the physical quantity of gold in which a definite nominal amount of money is redeemable. Money would still be kept nearly steady in general purchasing power. The commodity bundle defining the price index would in effect be the monetary standard, gold merely being the redemption medium. (Some other redemption medium might in fact be adopted as more convenient.)

By keeping the money unit always equal in value to the designated commodity bundle, two-way convertibility of the sort just described would go far — perhaps all the way — toward circumventing the problem of lags that so routinely forms an objection to targeting the management of irredeemable money on a price index. (That objection stresses lags between incipient money-supply-and-demand disequilibrium and its reflection in the price index and between index movements and policy responses and their corrective effects.)

If the United States and other countries joined in adopting index-targeted money units, they would largely eliminate any basis for wide exchange-rate swings unwarranted by economic "fundamentals." The same happy result would follow from the more thoroughgoing reform described earlier — specification of a unit of account, abolition of government money, and provision of media of exchange by private enterprise only. Even if only the United States abolished governmental discretion over money by adopting either of these reforms, the basis for unwarranted exchange-rate movements would be removed, on one side anyway.

It is on radical domestic monetary reform, then, that I pin my hopes for a healthier system of international monetary relations.

Although I do not know how to solve the problems of international banking and international debts, I should perhaps at least acknowledge them. I had hoped to learn their solution from Robert Weintraub, who was scheduled to speak in this lecture series next February but who met an untimely death last September. For now, I have only a few remarks on the topic.

The temptation is understandable to have governments and the International Monetary Fund bail out the banks and their debtors. Otherwise, grave repercussions from loan defaults are feared. On the other hand, a bailout now would reinforce signals already sent in the past, such as those that promoted the so-called recycling of the surpluses of oil-exporting countries, signals that encourage short-run-oriented decisions on lending and borrowing risk creating the need, or supposed need, for bigger and more heroic bailouts in the future. The dilemma is a genuine one, and I cannot confidently recommend what choice to make.

I do recommend watching the International Monetary Fund as an example of bureaucratic empire-building. When its original role as centerpiece of the fundamentally flawed Bretton Woods system collapsed, the Fund began seeking other functions. It has partly transformed itself into an international aid agency, poaching on the territory of its sister institution, the World Bank. Creating the Fund in the first place was a mistake, in my opinion; and I am sympathetic to proposals (such as by Milton Friedman)[8] that it now, however belatedly, be abolished.

Money is only part of the international economic order, so I would like to express a few thoughts on trade policy. Many calls for protectionism in the United States nowadays insist that things have changed since the era when classical economics seemed to recommend free trade. Classroom doctrines no longer apply. U.S. policy must be "realistic." Free trade is acceptable only if it is "fair trade."

One recent article taking this line is noteworthy for being written by the president of the United States Industrial Council, an organization supposedly dedicated to winning support for a free society and a market economy. Anthony Harrigan finds the United States "the target of *economic* warfare." "[T]he trade situation is a battle" whose "outcome will determine the standard of living and the national security of the American people." Foreign governments subsidize companies selling in the United States and even own some of them. Those companies may subordinate profit to market share. The Japanese are insular and cliquish and shirk their fair share of defense costs. Their government controls and plans almost every phase of the Japanese economy — so Harrigan thinks. Other nations also "treat trade as an offensive weapon. Around the world, barriers are put up to keep out American products, while imports come into the U.S. in a flood that threatens to swamp our industries." By the turn of the century, Harrigan says (quoting a Berkeley professor of political science), the combined industrial power of several Asian nations will exceed that of the United States or Western Europe. The upshot is that we desperately need "protection against foreign governments." We should "insist on measures to promote genuine free trade — fair trade — in international circles."[9]

Well, let's see. Suppose foreign governments do give their companies advantages allowing them to compete cheaply in the American market. Just how does it matter to us *why* Ruritanian widgets delivered in the United States are as cheap as they are? (I follow Ludwig von Mises in referring to the fictional Ruritania.) Perhaps Ruritania's climate and resources are ideal for widget production. Perhaps widgets grow wild on bushes and can be harvested at slight cost. Perhaps the Ruritanian industry enjoys the special skills that its workers have developed over generations. Perhaps a mass market in Ruritania affords scope for economies of large-scale production. Perhaps Ruritanian manufacturers are selling below current cost in an effort to expand sales and production, take advantage of the learning curve, and get costs down. Perhaps the Ruritanian government has been deliberately fostering a large and efficient widget industry. Perhaps Ruritanian employers scandalously underpay their workers. Perhaps the Ruritanian government subsidizes the dumping of widgets in the United States at below the home price or below the cost of production.

How does the particular reason for the cheapness of imported widgets condition their impact on the American economy? If cheap foreign goods either benefit or harm us Americans, how could the nature and degree of that benefit or harm hinge on something more recondite than the prices of the goods themselves? If detailed investigation of costs and prices in Ruritania would be necessary to determine whether so-called dumping is taking place, does not that very necessity show that the reason why the imports are so cheap cannot be inferred from effects observable in the United States?

Some answers might be given to these questions, but I challenge protectionists to face them squarely. Conceivably the reason why foreign goods are cheap might give a clue to how *dependable* their cheapness is. One or two theoretical-curiosity cases might also provide answers (see Yeager and Tuerck, pp. 149-54, 198-99, including the long footnote on

p. 199).[10] The point to stress, however, is that foreign goods available at low prices offer us Americans an opportunity for gain.

Similar remarks apply to complaints about government ownership of foreign companies selling in the United States. The burden of that socialism falls on foreign taxpayers, not on us Americans. If political and other factors make for inefficiency, swelling losses and requiring subsidies, or if private enterprise is restricted from competing with those companies in their home countries, it is primarily the foreigners who suffer. In the United States, socialized foreign companies cannot compel customers to do business with them and cannot forcibly exclude competitors. Since the disadvantages of socialism are concentrated on the countries practicing it, pointing to it with alarm, or, more broadly, pointing to government control and planning serves more as a debating point than as a substantive point. It stirs up emotions against tricky and unfair foreigners.

Mr. Harrigan's worry over the growth of wealth and productive capacity abroad would be relevant if the foreign countries were actual adversaries and not just metaphorical adversaries in a supposed contest of economic performance. Trade with the Soviet Union may benefit the Russians more than it benefits us, thereby strengthening them relatively in an actual struggle. This reason for wariness about trade with Russia does not apply, however, to trade with friendly or neutral countries.

We all sympathize with American workers displaced by the competition of cheap imports. Their displacement is what it is, however, regardless of just why the imports are cheap. American workers are no better or worse off if displaced by subsidized imports than if displaced by imports actually produced at low cost, displaced by competition at home, displaced by new and better products, or displaced by changes in the tastes of consumers.

Yet conjectured reasons for the cheapness of imports provide opportunities for deploying protectionist arguments appealing less to fact and analysis than to emotion, xenophobia, and garbled notions of morality. "Unfair!" is the cry, as if the foreigners were cheating in a game. "Fair competition" is an end in its own right in a game or a race, but not in trade. The objective of trade is to get goods on advantageous terms. To interfere with trade because foreigners offer us exceptionally advantageous terms is to reject the very principle of gain from trade. Complaints and action would be justified if foreign competitors were physically sabotaging American production or were spreading lies about the safety or quality of American products; not only the American producers but also their potential customers would then be suffering unfair victimization. The mere cheapness of foreign goods is emphatically *not* the same thing.

The economics of how to reply to standard complaints about "unfair" foreign competition is clear enough. The challenge is one of effective exposition — of how to get the message across to emotionally closed minds.

An economy with rising standards of living, improving job opportunities, and freedom for consumers and workers — and entrepreneurs and investors — to explore and cultivate the opportunities open to them is bound to be a world of change. Change always harms some people. In response to change, the choice lies between, on the one hand, institutions and policies that try either to block change or provide shelters against its impact and, on the other hand, institutions and policies that facilitate advantageously adjusting to it. The protectionist road leads to stagnation. The other road is that of a free-market economy, with flexible prices tending to promote market-clearing in the face of changed conditions and at the same time conveying appropriate signals and incentives.

The issue is a large one. It comes to its sharpest focus in the arena of foreign trade policy: What sort of economic system do we want? Do we want a free-market economy, the system most conducive to a society of free and prosperous men and women? Or do we want a politicized economy, pulled haphazardly this way and that by myriads of government interventions undertaken at the behest of special interests demanding protection from allegedly unfair competition? Do we really want the government to try to implement, somehow, someone's conception of a "fair" pattern of customer-supplier relations and a "fair" pattern of incomes? (On this question, I recommend Hayek's *The Constitution of Liberty*, chapter 6.)[11]

I hope that the men and women of Hillsdale College will champion the course recommended by Ludwig von Mises — free trade and sound money. (Of course, room for discussion remains on the best way of achieving sound money.) As I have tried to explain, safeguarding money from governmental ruination would contribute greatly to a healthy national and international economic order.

It may be that the ideal of free men, free markets, and sound money will never be fully achieved. Yet as F. A. Hayek has explained in a festschrift for Ludwig von Mises, even "unrealistic" ideals are worth pursuing.

It is not to be denied that to some extent the guiding model of the overall order will always be a utopia, something to which the existing situation will only be a distant approximation and which many people will regard as wholly impractical. Yet it is only by constantly holding up the guiding conception of an internally consistent model which could be realized by consistent application of the same principles, that anything like an effective framework for a functioning spontaneous order will be achieved.[12]

NOTES

[1] International Monetary Fund, *Annual Report 1983* (Washington: IMF, 1983), pp. 65–66.

[2] Alan Reynolds, "Gold and Economic Boom: Five Case Studies, 1792–1926," in *Money in Crisis*, Chap. 10 (San Francisco: Pacific Institute for Public Policy Research, 1984).

[3] Thomas de Vries, discussion in *Exchange Rate Flexibility*, ed. Jacob S. Dreyer, Gottfried Haberler, and Thomas D. Willett (Washington: American Enterprise Institute, 1978), pp. 191–92.

[4] Milton Friedman, "Real and Pseudo Gold Standards," *Journal of Law and Economics* 4 (1961), reprinted in his *Dollars and Deficits* (Englewood Cliffs: Prentice-Hall, 1968), pp. 247–65.

[5] F. A. Hayek, "The Future Monetary Unit of Value," in *Money in Crisis*, Chap. 13 (San Francisco: Pacific Institute for Public Policy Research, 1984).

[6] Robert L. Greenfield and Leland B. Yeager, "A Laissez-Faire Approach to Monetary Stability," *Journal of Money, Credit, and Banking* 15 (August, 1983), 302–15.

[7] Irving Fisher, *Stabilizing the Dollar* (New York: Macmillan, 1920).

[8] Milton Friedman, " 'No' to More Money for the IMF," *Newsweek* (November 14, 1983), p. 96.

[9] Anthony Harrigan, "Needed: A Strategic Economic Policy," *National Review* 35 (March 4, 1983), pp. 240–45.

[10] Leland B. Yeager and David G. Tuerck, *Trade Policy and the Price System* (Scranton: International Textbook Company, 1966).

[11] F. A. Hayek, *The Constitution of Liberty* (Chicago: University of Chicago Press, 1960).

[12] F. A. Hayek, "Principles or Expediency?," in *Toward Liberty* (festschrift for Ludwig von Mises), I (Menlo Park: Institute for Humane Studies, 1971), pp. 29–45.

Melvyn Krauss

Is Reagan Losing the
Battle of Ideas in the Third World?

Traditionally, the strongest voices for increased foreign economic aid to the poorer countries have been American liberals and European social democrats. The justifications for such aid have been varied. Western guilt for Third-World poverty has been cited by some. Others cite alleged distortions in the system of international capitalistic competition that work to the disadvantage of the less-developed countries (LDCs). Yet others claim the West has a moral duty to compensate for the alleged cultural and environmental inability of Third-World peoples to sustain adequate economic growth. And finally there are the global egalitarians who justify international income transfers on that simple-minded basis alone.

Conservatives, by and large, have done well in countering these arguments. They have understood that economics is not a "zero sum" game; that economic gain by one does not imply a corresponding economic loss by another. They have shown that the "terms of trade" between the have and have-less countries have not shown a secular decline against the poorer ones. They have witnessed the rapid economic growth of several less-developed countries, thus exposing the "inability of poorer countries to grow" thesis for the racist myth it, in fact, is. And they have had faith that the only type of equality that has value to Americans is equality of opportunity, not equality of outcomes.

Convincing arguments based on sound economic analysis and historical evidence have enabled conservatives in this country to keep liberal give-away tendencies in check. It is therefore ironic in the extreme that tradition currently is being stood on its head, that conservatives — not liberals — have become the strongest voice for massive transfers of income and wealth to poor countries, and that at the vanguard of this attempt to somersault economic logic and common sense is an administration in Washington that critics claim to be the most conservative this country has experienced in decades.

My morning *New York Times* (February 4, 1984), for example, boasts the headline, "President Asks $8 Billion in Aid for Latin America." "If we don't help now," the President is quoted as saying, "we'll surely pay dearly in the future." And as if to prove that political transvestitism is currently peaking in the nation's capital, liberal Congressman Clarence D. Long is quoted as saying that "we just don't have the money . . . It goes against the President's own program of cutting spending . . . They're asking for a huge increase in foreign aid in an area where the results of foreign aid have not been very reassuring." Mr. Reagan countered by telling Congressional leaders: "Our plan is for the long haul. It

won't be easy and it won't be cheap. But it can be done. And
for strategic and moral reasons it must be done."

The word to underline, of course, is *strategic*. Mr. Reagan
clearly is treating the $8 billion in economic aid as if it were a
defense expenditure. And when it comes to defense, there
appears to be no amount too high for this President to pay.

This is not to say that I disagree with the analysis of the
Kissinger Report on Central America that American security
interests "are importantly engaged" by a Soviet–Cuban
challenge in Central America. They most certainly are. Nor is
Dr. Kissinger mistaken, in my view, about the need for a
military response to help combat Soviet–Cuban aggression.
But where conservative "realists" like Mr. Reagan and Dr.
Kissinger go wrong is in their willingness to pay an extraordinarily high price to a consortium of special interests in the
U.S. — international bankers, American businessmen who
traffic in Central America, trade unionists and liberal politicians — to free the military weapons for use by our Central
American allies. Eight billion dollars in economic aid to
secure an increase of $400 million in increased military
assistance to Central America is a bad deal, even if the pack-
age were to prove an effective response to the Soviet-Cuban
threat. And one can almost guarantee it will not.

Compromise or Surrender

Reagan "realists" confuse surrender with compromise.
When our European allies threatened us with a "you adopt
detente or else we won't let you defend us" proposition in
the 1983 Euromissile crisis, the Reagan administration opted
for Atlantic unity on European terms rather than risk Euro-

pean rejection of the missiles. The "realists" and detentniks won. Now when Congressional liberals threaten the Reagan administration with "you promote social justice and help redistribute income in Central America or else we won't let you defend them," the Reagan "realists" have opted for solidarity with liberals rather than risk rejection of increased military spending. Once again, Ronald Reagan has surrendered his strategic principles in the hope of denying the Soviets a victory.

The tragedy of this is that "Reagan realism" will not work. For one, the President is ceding the "battle of ideas" to his opponents. In Central America, the liberals are convinced that leftist guerilla movements are caused by social injustice and a bad distribution of income. They advise we sponsor social welfare programs — schools, hospitals, agricultural reform — along with massive infusions of foreign economic aid to counter the guerillas.

As you know, the conservative diagnosis of Central American problems differs dramatically. Poverty is not caused by a bad income distribution or social injustice. Rather it results from bad government policies (often introduced in the name of social justice and distributive equity) that thwart economic growth — high taxes, protectionism, excessive government spending, politicized markets, debasement of the currency — and so on. To the extent that poverty provides fertile soil in which left-wing revolutionaries can thrive, these bad policies must be reversed. But conservatives are not necessarily economic determinists, and a good many are skeptical that poverty is that influential in promoting left-wing revolutions in the first place.

The *Kissinger Report* gives the liberals almost everything they want: it favors land reform, income redistribution, increased aid for education, infrastructure, health facilities, "human rights" conditions on military aid, and lots of foreign aid dollars. This is bad enough. But by advocating a social-democratic grab bag as medicine for the Soviet–Cuban disease, the *Kissinger Report* appears to justify — indeed endorse — the correctness of the liberal diagnosis of Third-World turbulence. Kissinger, the pragmatist, may see the economic aid merely as a payoff to liberals to dispatch the military hardware to Central America. But public opinion is more likely to interpret Ronald Reagan's embracing of the Kissinger proposals as an admission — by deed if not word — that social injustice has been the root cause of Central America's problems.

This is an extremely important setback for the conservative cause both for ideological and practical reasons. Ideologically, it strengthens the credibility of the liberal diagnosis of left-wing revolutions in the Third World. Practically, it strengthens Mr. Reagan's political opponents, so that if AFL–CIO chief Lane Kirkland's price for military aid to Central America seems high this time — $8 billion economic aid for $400+ million military — next time it will be even higher.

This is not the first time Reagan realists have engineered a Reagan defeat in the battle of ideas. The same thing happened when the Reagan administration chose to bail out international bankers and Third-World governments during the so-called international debt crisis. Reagan realists (such as Treasury Secretary Donald Regan) counseled a bailout through the IMF to avoid what they claimed would be an international financial panic, even though President Reagan apparently believes in the conservative diagnosis that unless Third-World borrowers are disciplined by the market for their mistakes in economic policy, and international banks disciplined for their cavalier lending practices, the debt problem is not likely to go away. On this occasion Ronald Reagan also failed to distinguish himself by behaving no differently than his liberal political opponents would have behaved under identical circumstances. And by failing to have the courage of his stated convictions against bailouts, administered by international bureaucrats, Reagan undermined both the credibility of these convictions and his own credibility in the public's eye.

Democracy and Prosperity

Mr. Reagan's ceding the battle of ideas to his opponents in Central America is extremely dangerous because a proper solution to that region's turbulence is vital to U.S. national security interests. It is one thing to have hostile regimes thousands of miles from our shores; another to have them on our front doorstep.

The United States has two clear interests in Central America. One is to promote *political democracy*; the other, to promote *economic prosperity*.

We should not underestimate the enormity of this task. Political democracy, in particular, is like a gem valued both for its beauty and scarcity. In truth, there are very few examples of working democracies in the poorer countries.

We must recognize the long-term nature of this objective and that there is a reasonable chance of failure. To insure ourselves in case of failure, the economic role that government plays in Central American societies should be scaled down. Political democracy, after all, refers to the political process, not the market system. The more things are done through the market system, and the less through the political process, the less relevant will be the failure to achieve political democracy, at least in a relatively short time. For example, popular control over the political process is much more important in a socialist society where government distributes, say, ninety percent of the national income than in a capitalistic society where it distributes, say, ten percent. There is simply more at stake in politics when economic life is highly politicized.

This is not to argue, of course, that political democracy is not a worthwhile objective. It most certainly is. Only we should be realistic as to our prospects for achieving it in regions of the world where traditions have run in opposite directions.

Happily, reducing the role that government plays in the nation's economic life also is an indispensable condition for promoting economic prosperity in poorer countries. In comparing East Germany with West Germany, North Korea with South Korea, Red China with Nationalistic China, Finland with the Soviet Union, and Canada with the United States, it is always the country with big government that has produced continuing poverty for its citizens, while that with small government has produced economic prosperity.

The singlemost prosperous region of the Third World during the past quarter century has been the Pacific Basin area. And the countries of this area, by and large, have allowed government to play a small role in their economic lives.

One conclusion, therefore, is inescapable: the United States must use its influence in Central America to reduce the role that Central American governments play in their society's economic life. We must promote the privatization of the Central American economies and discourage their socialization. The Pacific Basin area should be their model.

There are three ways the U.S. government can assist in this privatization process. First to encourage private industry in Central America, the United States must remove all protective barriers to exports from this region. Unrestricted and unconditional access to the U.S. market is the *sine qua non* for the economic survival of our neighbors to the South. And it increases the economic well-being of consumers in this country as well.

When Congress and the administration give in to special-interest groups and the American trade union movement that plead protection against Central American exports, in effect, they join the Soviets and Cubans in a silent conspiracy to undermine the United States in the hemisphere in which we live. If we keep their exports out of our country, can we expect them to keep the Communists out of theirs? The geopolitical consequences of protection against Central American exports have been grossly underestimated.

Second, to help privatize Central American economies, we must reduce—not increase—our economic aid to them. Foreign economic aid, it must be remembered, represents government-to-government income transfer. It increases the size of recipient governments and thus socializes — not privatizes — their economies. Experience indicates economic aid very seldom trickles down to the people whose hearts and minds we hope to favorably influence. Rather, aid increases corruption.

The February 20, 1984 *New York Times* reported that:

> United States economic assistance programs to Central
> America suffer from extensive mismanagement and cor-
> ruption, according to State Department audits and a
> Congressional study. Abuses cited in the reports include
> the illegal diversion of funds for private gain, fraudulent
> accounting procedures, and spending that never reached
> the people it was intended to help. There were no exact
> figures for the amount of money wasted or misused, but
> both Administration officials and Congressional investi-
> gators estimate that the total runs into millions of
> dollars annually.

Ronald Reagan promises to change that figure from millions
to billions. Foreign aid also reinforces the privileged positions
of elites whose policies, more often than not, are responsible
for the recipient country's sorry economic plight in the first
instance.

Dramatic examples where foreign aid encouraged bad
economic policies are Taiwan and South Korea. In both
countries, American economic aid financed and sustained
wealth-destroying protectionist and anti-private-capital import policies. So long as generous U.S. economic aid was
forthcoming, Taiwan and South Korea could forego private-
capital import and export promotion for foreign exchange
purposes. But when the aid was discontinued in the 1960s,
the generation of foreign exchange by the private sector became critical. It was not mere coincidence that both countries
radically altered their domestic economic policies from im-

port substitution to export-led growth in the face of the U.S. aid cutoff. It was cause and effect.

In addition to promoting economic stagnation, there were fears in Taiwan that the U.S. economic aid had made the country too dependent on the U.S. Independence from foreigners had been a central motif of Nationalist Chinese international economic policy since Sun Yat-sen. The result, as in many Third-World countries, was that Taiwan opted for protectionist policies in the early post-World War II period. An export-oriented, free-capital-import program was rejected precisely because it was seen as surrendering Taiwan's future development to private firms and foreign interests who, it was thought, would be preoccupied with profit and unresponsive to the political and historic imperatives President Chiang Kai-shek had defined for his island country.

Autarkic economic policies, however, did not bring independence. They brought the opposite. By running the economy into the ground, protectionism forced Taiwan to depend increasingly on the U.S. for general economic assistance. The Nationalist fear of dependence on private foreign firms thus led to the reality of "aid-dependency" on the U.S. In the final analysis, the Nationalist government realized that only the prosperous are truly independent, and that Chiang's earlier fear of foreign capital had been misplaced if not counter-productive.

From a U.S. point of view, it is dubious in the extreme that our national security is enhanced by financing government policies in the Third World that damage their economies. At some point the chickens come home to roost and we get regimes that are hostile to us — to wit, Iran and Nicaragua. Stripped of its rhetoric, foreign economic aid is little more than a mechanism for buying elites and preserving the status quo. That is not good enough for the millions of Central Americans who want the type of change that will bring them a better life. And it also should not be good enough for the United States whose traditions and current national security interests dictate that such change be supported.

President Reagan probably is correct when he says, "If we don't help now, we'll surely pay dearly in the future." But the way to help Central America is by *trade* not aid! The foreign aid route means that the Central Americans will take our money and resent us for it.

Indeed, there already is considerable criticism south of the border of the Kissinger proposal to make the foreign aid conditional upon the undertaking of certain economic reforms in recipient countries. According to a report in *The Wall Street Journal*, Costa Rica's Finance Minister Frederico Vargas "sees a danger that if the U.S. comes in here and says, 'We will give you this if you do this and that', it could be viewed as an invasion by the U.S. of our affairs." And Mexico's president Miguel de la Madrid is quoted in *The New York Times* that "industrialized countries must come to the aid of developing countries to improve their living conditions, but must do so without placing ideological restrictions on their aid. The major powers must respect the right of self-determination of the people."

Some may see this desire of Central Americans to divorce conditionality from the aid program as no Latin *quid* for Yankee *quo*. But if the president of the United States insists on putting *himself* over a barrel, it is not surprising that others try to take advantage of it. Paying $8 billion to be allowed the privilege of defending the recipients is what I call putting yourself over a barrel.

The third way the U.S. can help privatize the economies of Central America is to promote political stability there. One does not have to be a professional economist to understand that political stability is a necessary condition for economic prosperity; without it, businessmen will not invest, lenders will not lend, and foreign capital will not flow in. The sad truth is that as long as the Central American economies are externally threatened by Soviet-sponsored aggression, economic progress will not be possible.

The Kissinger response to the Soviet–Cuban challenge to political stability in the region is to propose an unhappy trade-off: more weapons for more corruption, more stagnation and more resentment of Uncle Sam. Given Ronald Reagan's leadership — or lack thereof — perhaps this was the best Dr. Kissinger could do. But clearly it is not good enough.

One Grenada is worth ten *Kissinger Reports* and costs one-tenth the price. The Kissinger trade-off should be rejected and replaced by alternative military responses to our enemies in the Grenadan mold. Why not go to the source, whether that source be Nicaragua or Cuba? At least a Grenadan-style response promises a chance of success, while all the *Kissinger Report* promises is that next time around the terms of trade will be even more adverse to our side — that is, we will get more corruption, waste and resentment for even fewer guns.

Would the American people support a generalized application of the Grenada approach in Central America? They supported it in Grenada. And if there is one thing that succeeds in this country, it is success. The bottom line of the *Kissinger Report* is that it reflects the "politics of failure." It is both a result and future cause of Ronald Reagan's losing the battle of ideas in the Third World. The Grenada approach, on the other hand, reflects the "politics of success." How realistic can the Reagan realists be when, given this choice between success and failure, they chose the latter?

Kurt R. Leube

On "The Denationalization of Money"

I am greatly honored to have been invited to this distinguished institution and to have been given the opportunity to address you. I have been a guest in your wonderful and open-minded country for some five months now, and am truly coming to appreciate the values for which your college stands. I have seen that an ordered system of individual liberty is not, as so many in Europe, especially in the German-speaking world, believe, an attempt to maintain not a theory without applicability in modern society, but rather the only theory which can allow such a society to function for the good of all.

Although this is my first visit to your campus, our paths have crossed already in an interesting and, to some extent, significant episode which I would like to relate to you briefly here. Sometime, maybe eleven years ago, when I was still involved on a daily basis in the somewhat frustrating fight for liberalism in Austria with my honored teacher, F. A. von Hayek, a letter from Mrs. Margit von Mises appeared in the mail at our department at the University of Salzburg, offering for sale the library of her late husband, Ludwig von Mises. Since all our universities are state institutions, we were forced to direct our desire to purchase this outstanding collection, in order to combine it with F. A. von Hayek's own personal library, to the responsible bureaucrats of the Ministry for Science, Research and Culture.

I am absolutely sure that I don't have to explain to you the reasons why the Austrian "social-democratic" authorities showed very little interest in our request for money. Although our disappointment at the time was great, in retrospect, I am gratified to see the library of this genius residing here at an institution where its worth is appreciated by the faculty and the student body. This gratification is only magnified by the knowledge that the priceless and unique Hayek library of some 7,000 volumes, with which he was forced to part for financial reasons upon assuming a visiting professorship at the University of Salzburg, now stands collecting dust in an annex to the poor library of that institution.

Now, let me turn to my topic by beginning with a brief historical sketch of the important contributions of the Austrian School to the development of a "monetary equivalent of a free society." It is often argued that the contributions of the Austrian School of Economics to monetary theory consist only of a somewhat mechanical attempt to apply the marginal utility theory to the problems of the value of money. I don't agree with this claim, for the Austrian School's contribution was much more extensive.

I shall outline here the history of these important contributions, especially the discussions at the 1892 "Kuk Austro-Hungarian Currency Committee" of which Carl Menger, the founder of the Austrian School, was one of the most eminent members. Besides Menger, there participated others who, well known then within the tradition of the Austrian School, have been forgotten in recent years: Emil Sax (1845-1927), an authority in public policy theory; Victor Mataja (1857-1933), an expert in public finance; Richard Lieben, who was eventually not to be counted as an "Austrian" and who tried to apply the marginal utility theory into mathematical form; and, as a government representative, the famous Eugen von Boehm-Bawerk (1851-1914), the leading figure of the second generation of the Austrian School.

The tasks of this commission were to discuss the basis of a future currency, existing silver and paper circulation, the ratio of exchange between the existing paper and growth, and the nature of a new unit to be adopted. Menger's and Boehm-Bawerk's mastery of the problems, no less than their gift of clear exposition, gave them immediately a leading position in the commission, and their statements attracted the public. Their statements even caused a slight temporary slump on the Viennese Stock Exchange.

I have to confine myself to sketching briefly only Menger's contributions. They consist of an interesting and careful discussion of the theoretical problems of the exact parity to be chosen between different currencies. Menger also evaluated the practical difficulties which occur with any transition to a newly developed standard of currency, but he did not solve these most important problems. Furthermore, I found his distinction between the "inner" and the "outer" value of money somewhat misleading.

In those days, long since gone, at least in Austria, it was for the first time that members of the first and second generation of the Austrian School fought together for a kind of monetary equivalent to a free society. But Menger made his most powerful contributions to the problem of the value of money in the last chapter of his *Principles of Economics*,[1] and also in his not very well-known articles on money, neither of which to my knowledge are available in English. Until the tremendous work some twenty years later of Ludwig von Mises, whose genius and intellectual power we are honoring with these lectures, and who to some extent continued Menger's earlier efforts, those articles in my opinion remained the main contribution of the Austrian School to the monetary theory.

Again, some twenty years later, it was Richard von Strigl (1891–1942), an eminent, though lesser-known scholar in the Austrian tradition, who, in an almost forgotten essay,[2] suggested that one way to restrain government abuse of the currency is to allow individuals to contract among themselves in any currency they choose. Strigl suggested that those contracts should be enforced by law. This proposal to my knowledge is the first statement in the tradition of the Austrian School advocating a kind of "choice in currency."

Now, some forty-five years later, my admired teacher F. A. von Hayek has published his "monetary revolution" entitled *The Denationalization of Money*.[3] I am going to try to explain what that means and shall follow his arguments.

In advocating a free-enterprise "solution," namely the right of individuals to create money, everybody should be free to offer money of different denominations or different kinds to the general public. This sounds somewhat utopian, but it would be the market that would decide ultimately which of these monies would become generally accepted. The new feature of Hayek's proposal will be clear when one realizes that in the big debates on free banking or the free issue of money, most of the scholars were talking about private institutions issuing existing currencies. But, such a situation would create only deprivations of these currencies and could lead to inflation.

If private institutions could create their own distinctive currency, backed by whatever they choose, the general public would immediately know with whose currency they are dealing. It is to be expected that there would develop a real market situation like the market for, say, any given consumer good. A private institution which has to issue money in competition with other issuers can only remain in business if it provides the public with a fairly stable money in which they can trust. Any form of distrust which may arise regarding the issuer abusing his position would immediately lead to the reaction of the market, and thus, to a depreciation of his unit, driving him out of the market. The market power will be by far a better disciplining force than any state interventionism, or even a legal framework. Over a certain span of time people will adjust themselves to this kind of new situation.

After World War II in Germany, it took people not more than a few days to adjust themselves to the so-called "Zigarettenwaehrung." As far as I know, a similar phenomenon is also to be observed in Poland at the present time. The creation of a government monopoly in monetary matters, however, is clearly no longer a viable solution to the problem of a stable money.

What traits should characterize good money? On which standards should it be based? If there is to be a "choice in currency," the different units have to be backed by different standards, whether they are backed by hard commodities that cannot be inflated easily, or by metals that have relatively low transaction cost. Although Hayek considered the gold standard as an almost ideal means to prevent governments from abusing their powers by inflating the national currencies, respectively,[4] the relying upon only one unit would prevent us from finding out what kind of money would best fit our needs. The gold standard, for example, specifies that a given unit of gold is vested with the ability to clear a debt of a given monetary value. This standard is and was favored only because it provides an effective protection from government abuse of its monopoly to issue money. But such a monopoly has the defect of all monopolies—that one must use their product even if it is unsatisfactory. Above all, it prevents the discovery of better methods of satisfying a need for which a monopolist has no incentive.[5]

Ever since the right of coinage was declared one of the essential attributes of sovereignty, the contention has been that government needed power to supply itself with money. And yet, there have been just a few attempts to justify these monopolies on grounds that it would provide any better money. Should we, therefore, look for a money which keeps its value in relation to all other commodities, or some? What should we expect from good money? People prefer to use money as a medium of exchange over other commodities because it possesses a greater degree of liquidity. Liquidity may be defined as the capacity to fulfill financial obligations, and is not identical with cash reserves. This is what indeed distinguishes money from commodities. Following Menger, only the market process promoted a single commodity, namely gold, to the status of a most liquid commodity. Thus has gold become money. Money as such has not been created by the state; it is a social institution.

Commodities may stay stable in their values in normal times and, if we are not being forced to sell them too fast, different monies may have the same degree of liquidity though differing in stability. Thus, the basic premise on which most of the argument rests is that if people were free to choose which money they desired to use in their daily transactions, it would probably lead to a preference for that money having a fairly stable purchasing power.

Normally the argument runs as follows: a good money should be nearly stable in terms of purchasing power. That means that this money should be approximately constant in terms of its average prices. But the prices of some goods change dramatically because they function as market signals in order to inform us about unknown and unexpected events. This, however, is in contrast to people's desire for a medium which is able to reduce the uncertainty of future price changes.

As Hayek argues, the uncertainty about future prices can be minimized if the risk of making mistakes in anticipating future price changes, because the effects of errors in opposite directions will tend to cancel each other out. This cancelling will not take place if the median around which the deviation of individual prices clusters is not zero but some unknown magnitude.[6] That means that a stable money, through which the price of any commodity about which we have no information, would be as likely to rise as to fall, with the result of each balancing the other. In other words, a stable level in average prices creates circumstances in which a rise or fall in the money price of any commodity would indicate that it has risen or fallen in price, relative to most other commodities too. Therefore, it will not become relatively cheaper or more expensive than most other goods or commodities whose prices have decreased or increased.[7]

A money which keeps its purchasing power and its average price at a constant level may be able to distort the whole structure of relative prices. Thus, any changes in the quantity of money can cause unforeseen fluctuations in the relative price structure for a period of time as long as the increase in the money quantity continues. Changes in money prices never reach all commodities at the same time, and they will not affect the prices of the various goods to the same extent. Shifts in relationship between the demand for and the quantity of money for cash holdings generated by changes in the value of the money will not appear uniformly throughout any growing economy where prices sometimes have a tendency to fall. In order to keep them constant, the quantity of money must increase, which can lead to the distortion of the structure of relative prices. This insoluble problem concerns the notion of "neutral money" which Prof. Hayek described in length in his fascinating 1933 essay entitled "Ueber Neutrales Geld."[8] If money were neutral in its effects, it would not affect the allocatable mechanism.

Within Hayek's denationalization proposal, each issuer would have his own unit, and not competing currencies based on one and the same "standard." Thus, the different units would fluctuate freely against all other units (and standard?). All of which leads me to the brief discussion of the "legal tender" problem. A consequence of being able to choose different currencies would not only be that the public would prefer to handle their obligations in a currency they could trust, but also that they eventually would accept any currency for payment for their goods and services. They would be able to change the unit quickly, if they did not trust the chosen one anymore. There is no doubt that a "choice in currency" would be much more inventive in providing the sort of money needed for the proper function of markets. There is no need for legal tender at all. The term legal tender was understood as government forcing parties into a contract to discharge their financial obligations in a certain form that people had not intended when they concluded their contract.

And as far as the famed "Gresham's Law" is concerned, meaning that bad money will drive out good money, this will not apply. This "law" does not apply to competing money of different denominations whose rate of exchange between which is determined by the market. It does apply to different monies that have a fixed exchange rate enforced by the government. Where the relative value of money is determined by the market, the opposite is true and has been proven for many different historical periods.

How would it work internationally? It would depend upon the success or failure of the competing international units, which as such may be based on different standards. That means, there could be considerable differences between the different commodities to which the monetary "index" is stuck. It should be clear that the idea is far from any solution and very provisional. The question of choosing the commodities which would become the standard for assessing the average purchasing power, not just in certain regions, is to be solved.

Thus we have to look for a fairly stable international standard, which could be the wholesale prices of, say, a portfolio of five or more different metals. Those metals cannot easily be inflated, and have relatively low transaction, storage, and transportation cost. Such a portfolio is not supposed to be vulnerable to big swings in just one market. A portfolio of five or more different countries, where free trade in precious metals is allowed, should be chosen, and at the beginning five or more internationally operated banks should be trusted with the development of such an international private currency. In the long run, some different standards would prevail, perhaps worldwide. But the transactions cost would still remain very high, a fact which obviously cannot be neglected. There are, of course, several other externalities involved, such as confidence externalities and price-level externalities.

There is just one single test procedure to find out whether our current money system is more efficient than one of currency competition, and whether or not governments are the most efficient providers of the common monies compared to an alternative system which would allow the public a "choice in currency." Since "the monopoly of government in issuing money . . . has . . . deprived us of the only process by which we can find out what would be good money,"[9] such a "competition as a discovery procedure" might even have advantages if the process would be known to converge to the money created by the government, because nobody knows in advance to which kind of unit to converge.

I cannot raise here the many other consequences of such a proposal for a currency competition. It seems to me that the emergence of a newly invented, fairly stable international value unit that is not dependent on the government's will would have quite more far-reaching consequences than at first glance. The whole radical proposal requires the removal of ingrained habits. It took more than one generation from the publication of Menger's *Principles* until his approach became widely accepted. Thus, in my opinion, another span of time might be needed to get this fascinating, highly complex, and exciting approach to work.

NOTES

[1] Carl Menger, *Grundsaetze der Volkswirtschaftslehre*, Chapter 8 (Vienna: 1871).
[2] Richard von Strigl, "Gibt es eine Sicherung gegen Inflation?," *Mitteilungen oesterreichischer Banken und Bankiers*, XV, No. 6 (1932).
[3] F. A. von Hayek, *Denationalization of Money, The Argument Refined*, Hobart Paper 70 (London: The Institute of Economic Affairs, 1978).
[4] F. A. von Hayek, *Monetary Nationalism and International Stability* (Geneva: The Graduate Institute of International Studies, 1937).
[5] Hayek, *Denationalization of Money*, p. 24.
[6] *Ibid.*, p. 70.
[7] Alex Bilimovic, "Kritische und positive Bemerkungen zur Geldwerttheorie," *Zeitschrift fuer Nationaloekonomie*, II, No. 3 (1931).
[8] F. A. von Hayek, "Ueber Neutrales Geld." *Zeitschrift fuer Nationaloekonomie*, IV, No. 5 (1933).
[9] F. A. von Hayek, "Towards a Free Market Monetary System," *Journal of Libertarian Studies* (1978), 5.

Anthony Harrigan

International Trade Policy: Is There Such a Thing?

The topic of my discussion is "International Trade Policy: Is There Such a Thing?" I have a convenient answer to that question: yes and no. Yes, a number of countries have well-thought-out trade policies. No, the United States hasn't a clear-cut policy; instead it has a grab bag of policies.

Note: I wasn't asked to defend or repudiate any particular trade policy. I wasn't asked to praise one theory of trade or condemn another theory. I was simply asked, " Is there such a thing as international trade policy?" Phrased as such, this question, then, gives me an opportunity to conduct a wide-ranging exploration.

In my view, the most spectacular example of an international trade policy, one which works, is offered by Japan. As Dr. Andrea Boltho of Magdalen College, University of Oxford, said in an address at the University of the South (March, 1984), Japan's share in world exports of manufactures rose by 15 percentage points per annum in the 30 years to 1983, and, as a result, "Japan entered the technological competition of the 1980s as a direct rival to the strongest economy of the world — that of the United States." This strong position was achieved by design, by national consensus, by a unique combination of trade and industrial policies. First, it was achieved through an extensive network of old-style strict protection, then by the very Japanese method of administrative guidance which, in Dr. Boltho's words, included "notifications, recommendations, instructions, directives, wishes, opinions."

Now I submit that it is the unstated but real trade and industrial policy of Japan to strive to dominate the American domestic market for automobiles, steel, semi-conductors and many other products. Operating through the Ministry of International Trade and Industry (MITI), the Japanese map trade offensives, conduct research in government agencies, select the companies involved in trade offensives, provide cheap credit, and coordinate the overseas operations of giant industrial firms as though they were field armies. All this has been fully documented in business journals and U.S. government reports.

This policy has been in effect since the 1950s and has been extraordinarily successful. The U.S. response to these national economic offensives — virtual economic warfare — has been repeated expressions of dedication to the principles of free trade.

In April of 1984, Secretary of the Treasury Donald Regan again stressed that Japan restricts foreign investment in yen-dominated assets and restricts the outflow of yen from Japan. U.S. trade representative William Brock said trade with Japan is increasingly a "one-way street," and added: "I've heard the Japanese equivalent of manana about as much as I can handle." He warned that the Japanese are tempting fate by their obduracy.

Let's be very clear about the Japanese system which has brought about so much economic distress and soul-searching in the United States in recent years. There are hundreds of accounts of this system; all explain that it involves a protected home market, but a competitive one so that there isn't the stagnation that free traders say is inevitable. By the way, one of the leading opponents of a *fair* trade policy (in March, 1984, he warned of a "debilitating trade war") is Hobart Rowen, editorial page commentator on economics for the liberal *Washington Post*. This is a reminder that liberals and conservatives are to be found on *both sides of the trade policy issue*. In contradistinction to Mr. Rowen, Robert Kuttner of *The New Republic* takes an opposing position. He notes that:

> *The Japanese government, in close collaboration with industry, targets sectors for development.* It doesn't try to pick winners blindfolded; it creates them. It offers special equity loans, which need be repaid only if the venture turns a profit. It lends public capital through the Japan Development Bank, which signals private bankers to let funds flow. Where our government offers tax deductions to all businesses as an entitlement, Japan taxes ordinary business profits at stiff rates and saves its tax subsidies for targeted ventures. The government sometimes buys back outdated capital equipment to create markets for newer capital. The

famed Ministry of International Trade and Industry has pursued this essential strategy for better than twenty years, keeping foreign borrowers out of cheap Japanese capital markets, letting in foreign investors only on very restricted terms, moving Japan up the product ladder from cheap labor-intensive goods in the 1950s to autos and steel in the 1960s, consumer electronics in the early 1970s, and computers, semiconductors, optical fibers, and just about everything else by 1980. *The Japanese government also waives antimonopoly laws for development cartels, and organizes recession cartels when overcapacity is a problem.* And far from defying the discipline of the market, MITI encourages fierce domestic competition before winnowing the field down to a few export champions.

That, in my view, is a very accurate description of the Japanese system.

The system is not confined to Japan, however. *The Wall Street Journal* said April 13, 1984, that:

Like the Japan of the 1960s, Korea uses import restrictions to protect its infant industries. It targets likely exports, such as TV sets, sometimes at levels below production costs, to establish a foothold in other countries. This tactic frequently raises charges of illegal "dumping." The economy is centrally directed. A government-drafted five-year development plan charts the way for Korea's nine huge industrial conglomerates. There is also a conscious government policy to hold wages down to help make exports competitive.

While this system was in formation and operation, the United States sought — with some exceptions — to maintain a traditional free-trade policy. In that period of three decades, according to the *World Press Review* (July, 1983), the U.S. share of the global GNP fell from sixty percent in 1950 to 23.7 percent in 1980. In this connection, it is worthwhile noting that 20 years ago the U.S. imported $7 billion in manufactured goods. In 1982, it imported $143 billion.

The U.S. is the only major Western industrial nation to lose market share since 1970. American economic growth not only lagged behind Japan and the ambitious states of East Asia, but also behind France, West Germany and even Italy. Between 1970 and 1980, the U.S. share of global export trade dropped from 17.3 percent to 12.9 percent. The U.S. also has not been able to keep other nations from penetrating its own domestic market. In 1970, the U.S. still had a $5.4 billion trade surplus, but this turned into a $69.5 billion trade deficit in 1983, up 92 percent from the previous year. Economic Data Resources Inc. predicts that the trade deficit "could hit $174 billion by 1990." It's no wonder that many Americans are alarmed.

Dr. Stephen Cohen of the University of California told the American Textile Manufacturers Institute on March 15, 1984:

> The situation of U.S. industry is, in my opinion, terrifying. I am an alarmist, and not in just a small handful of industries, the losers. It covers the whole range: high-tech, middle-tech, low-tech, no-tech, ordinary products, exotic products, consumer goods, producer goods. We are running a trade deficit now of over $100 billion a year.

We have only to look around us, on our streets, in our homes and in our factories, to appreciate how successful Japanese trade policy has been over several decades. The other side of the coin is the failure of U.S. trade policy with respect to Japan. American companies have the greatest difficulty in even being allowed to sell in Japan, let alone invest in Japan.

Now I would *not* suggest that the United States attempt to copy Japanese procedures and set up an American Ministry of International Trade and Industry. We are a very different people. However, I *do* believe that it is imperative that we review and reevaluate what passes for trade policy in the United States — and the ideas which govern U.S. policy.

As we all know, the United States has long adhered to the ideal of free trade, and it is a worthy idea. Unfortunately, the conditions of free trade simply don't exist in the world today. Other nations don't subscribe to the concept. Despite this, we continue to light candles before the alter of free trade. We are repeatedly admonished from all quarters — *The Wall Street Journal* to the *Village Voice* — that any departure from our current trade posture would be a shift to protectionism, which is characterized as an unspeakable evil. We also are warned about the danger of a "trade war" if we oppose international trade practices as they apply to us. We hear the words: Remember Smoot-Hawley, as though the conditions of 1984 were the conditions that existed fifty years ago.

Only a very few commentators are willing to risk the opprobrium involved in questioning adherence to free-trade ideas in the face of changed global trade practices. One of these, Stanley J. Modic, the staunchly conservative editor of

Industry Week, has had the temerity to say that "free trade" is an ideology, not a reality.

I think that Americans, especially those who consider themselves conservatives, should give consideration to his position — indeed, the position I have come to agree with — that the United States has accepted what amounts to a unilateral free-trade system. Instead of greeting this statement with irritation, as though a cherished dogma had been violated, I believe conservatives should look to the *realities* of trade as they affect the American people and pay less attention to textbook propositions.

One of the ideas basic to free trade is that if you are more efficient at making soap, and I am better at making cloth, it would be absurd for both of us to produce the same goods. The wiser policy, according to this theory, is for each to do what he does best. Each, in other words, has some comparative advantage.

But that homely lesson doesn't accurately describe how the world economy works these days. Comparative advantage in our time isn't created by markets or climatic factors or whatever, but by government actions — such as the multibillion-dollar European subsidy for the airbus or Korea's $3 billion investment in a giant steel mill.

To quote Dr. Cohen again:

> There is a new game in the industrialized world and basically it is played against the U.S. and a few Western European nations. Japan invented the game. We call it in the trade the development state of state-centered trading strategies. Here among other things the govern-

ment is no longer the famous referee of U.S. economic theory, the way it says in the textbook. It's a player. Frankly it is also the coach, the quarterback, the blocking back and the front line.

There are Americans who say that we should let foreign competition, including foreign government capital infusion and government research and trade direction, take its course — that the principle of free trade must be preserved no matter what the objective condition. They would have U.S. consumers enjoy short-term opportunities at the expense of a devastated American industrial base.

Robert Kuttner (in the *New Republic*, March 28, 1983) says that free-trade purists think in these terms:

> If they (the foreign producers) are superior at making autos, TV's, tape recorders, cameras, steel, machine tools, baseballs, semiconductors, computers, and other peculiarly Oriental products, it is irrational to shelter our own benighted industries. Far more sensible to buy their goods, let the bracing tonic of competition shake America from its torpor, and wait for the market to reveal our niche in the international division of labor.

What is that niche? Indeed *is* there a niche? The truth is that most basic industrial goods can be produced almost anywhere on the globe, but with workers who are employed at vastly different wage levels.

Every developing country is attempting to emulate Japan, and some are doing so very successfully, notably Korea. Brazil and Mexico are among the countries that have invested enormous sums in steel production — all aimed at the U.S. market. As a result, we are getting a global glut of manufactured goods; and the pressure is on many governments to keep producing and keep exporting to the U.S., in order to keep employment up and the people quiet.

There are many disturbing ramifications of this situation. A sizeable percentage of U.S. purchasing power is going to create jobs overseas. True, many of our factories are more productive and efficient now than 10 years ago, but the foreign producers still have enormous wage advantages. Their authoritarian governments are in a position to keep a lid on wages. At the same time, national resources are used to buy the most modern equipment and duplicate it at home. American manufacturers find their goods produced in the U.S. to be too costly for their market, and they turn to offshore production in Mexico, Taiwan, Indonesia and elsewhere. And the money received by foreign producers doesn't come back to the U.S. in terms of purchases of American-manufactured goods — only raw materials. The Japanese National Railways, for example, have a rule against use of equipment produced abroad. They want to sell more and buy less from Uncle Sam, except in a few specialized fields. At the same time, the foreign producers are striving to develop their most advanced, high-tech goods. High tech is *not* an out or a refuge for us.

Free-trade purists continue to insist, however, that trade "is always in two directions." This is true but simplistic. One of the trade partners may end up with the short end of the stick. That's done even within one country. That was the case in trade between the North and the South in the U.S. from 1865 to the 1940s. That's our situation today. And our losses are not simply in what are described as older industries.

Dennis Carney, chairman of Wheeling Pittsburgh Steel Corp., has said, "Within the next several years, industries such as computers, air frames, telecommunications and space technology could be damaged more than our steel and auto industries are being damaged today." Truly, it is an across-the-board situation.

I have said that high tech is not an out for the United States. Let me give some supporting statements.

Philip Caldwell, chairman and CEO of the Ford Motor Co., made this point in a recent issue (November 7, 1983) of *Business Week*. "Let there be no mistake," he said, " 'the post-industrial economy' is a myth. The harvest of a brave new high-tech world cannot uphold the U.S. standard of living or its security. Nor can this enormous nation survive if its work force does nothing more than get up each morning to press one another's pants."

Mr. Caldwell is not the only prominent business leader to speak out in criticism of the notion that the United States can live by high tech and services industries alone. W. R. Timken, Jr., chairman of The Timken Co., has stressed the fundamental importance of basic industry to the well-being of the United States. In a very perceptive address, Mr. Timken spoke of "media mesmerization" in the talk of the "collapse of the American manufacturing industry and the rite of passage into the new information society." As long as the wealth is created through production, he said, "new jobs in other areas such as service can be supported." He remarked that "manufacturing generates more than twice as much activity as financial . . . No wonder other nations want to take over manufacturing from us . . . Imagine the negative result if a much larger amount of our industrial goods were to be imported. Of course, some will say new types of exports will offset increased imports. I believe this is pie-in-the-sky talk."

These are important statements by people who are involved with the realities of American business and industry. They aren't theorists. They understand that we can't let a global market ease us out of heavy industries in which the newly industrialized countries have an advantage — so that the U.S. will gain a comparative advantage in high-tech industries. The same factors that bear on the American steel industry bear on the electronics industries. You will recall Atari's decision to move operations from California to Hong Kong. And we cannot lower American wages to compete with those in the countries of Asia, not without experiencing a political explosion in the United States.

I submit that to survive in an era of foreign state-directed competition, the United States needs both more modernization and restrictions on imports. This has been the case with the U.S. textile industry, which many people would like to treat as geriatric and expendable. Six billion dollars have gone into investment in U.S. textiles in recent years, and productivity growth has been second only to electronics. But U.S. textiles face the heaviest competition from China, where the wage scale is 21 cents an hour. By the way, the U.S. industry is very competitive domestically.

Now the question, as I see it, is what should be done? Or what is to be our trade policy in the years ahead? To answer those questions, I would begin with an examination of *reality*, with an examination of *specific industries* and their *condition* and *prospects*. Many are in deep trouble. I shall cite only one — the machine tool industry, where imports have soared from 10.6 percent in 1972 to 33.8 percent in 1983. In the case of high-tech machining tools, more than three fourths of the machining centers and 60 percent of the numerically controlled lathes sold in the first half of 1983 were imports. What does that mean? Stanley Modic warns that, "Displacement of domestic machine tool production capacity by factories in Japan and Europe would seriously jeopardize the U.S. defense capability."

For my own part, I don't encounter any intellectual obstacles in responding to this problem. My views about our country and its system are, generally, of the Russell Kirk variety, that is, a conservatism mindful of the community and national interest and national security. I don't subscribe to the view that we must begin our commitment to society with an ideology or theory. Instead, I think in terms of our inheritance of freedom and also our material inheritance in this country. Capitalism existed and flourished before theories were developed about it. A measure of economic nationalism, therefore, strikes me as completely normal and in line with our traditions, beginning with Alexander Hamilton and his concern for our infant industries.

Other Americans approach the subject of international trade from a very different perspective. The libertarian, like the liberal, seems to be wedded to the notion of one economic world. The traditional conservative, however, always has his mind on the *national* interest.

Dr. William Hawkins of the Radford University department of economics wrote a brilliant paper this winter which dealt with this subject. The following is a quotation from this paper which bears on the point I am making—the increased economic nationalism which I favor for the United States. He said:

There is a need to be concerned about the distribution of industry, wealth, employment and power among national groups. This makes for a major schism between classical liberals and nationalists. In contravention to the claims of idealists, the world is likely to remain divided into competing nation-states for quite some time. Diversity fostered by history and culture is reinforced by politics and ideology. Thus the term "world market" has little more meaning than the terms "world opinion" or "world government." International trade is not harmonious; it is competitive with very high stakes. One can accept the validity of classical principles and still wish to place prudent limits on the extent to which policies are based on them. The Founding Fathers placed the commerce clause in the Constitution to ensure an open domestic market free from barriers to internal trade which might be erected by the various States, but at the same time did not rule out national barriers to trade. Prominent advocates of national economic advancement, such as Alexander Hamilton, saw no contradiction in arguing for both internal freedom and external restrictions.

To return for a moment to the original question assigned to me, "Is there such a thing as international trade policy?," let me also quote (for I think it is appropriate) what Benjamin Disraeli, the British conservative statesman, had to say on the subject of trade policy. "Free trade," he said, "is not a rule, it is an expedient . . . Protection is not a rule, it is an expedient." And bear in mind, an expedient is defined as something that's characterized by suitability, practicality and efficiency in achieving a particular end. Isn't that what we want in an international trade policy? We are trying to deal with a trade problem that, in the words of *Business Week*, could turn out to be the "economic disaster of the decade."

I want to make clear that I am talking about the threatened *deindustrialization* of the United States, for that is what will take place if large industries go under as a result of state-directed foreign competition. Many people find it hard to imagine a deindustrialized United States. They should take a look at some of the industrial wasteland areas in the Middle West — Cleveland and Chicago — or at some of the new industrial plants, now shut down, in Sunbelt areas. A deindustrialized United States would be poor, weak and vulnerable to pressure and/or attack from its foes. We cannot permit industrial deterioration to continue in this country. And let me stress again that I am talking about the most advanced industries. As the Coalition for International Trade Equity said recently (and that's DuPont, Monsanto, Cincinnati Milicron, United Technologies Corp., etc.), "The adverse effects for the United States of foreign targeting efforts are already evident in the serious erosion of U.S. jobs, world market shares, and financial performance of the United States, including robotics, semi-conductors, telecommunications equipment and aircraft."

I hope that this exploration of international trade policy makes sense. I have reached my position as a result of awareness of the plight of many American companies, their shareholders, managers and employees — and the communities where they operate. I don't believe that things can continue

as they are. I am profoundly dismayed by ritual praise for
free trade in light of the militant state trade strategies in
place around the world. To date, much of the public debate
over international trade seems to miss the mark. There are
the protectionist extremists who demand domestic content
legislation without trying other remedies. And there are my
free-trade friends who seem to favor benign neglect, or what
they regard as benign neglect — a rundown of our industrial
base that they believe will produce good results in the end.

I should insert here that I believe, to some degree, debates
over international trade policy in our country have taken on
the passionate character of sectarian debates in another era.
Ideas often seem to be held because they are articles of faith,
perhaps even a dogma. There is a place for dogmatic tenets in
religion, but I seriously question the place of them in address-
ing economic realities. And it is the realities to which we
should address ourselves. We should *never* lose sight of them.
Our eyes should not be on theories on the printed page but
on conditions in factories and other workplaces. We need to
ask ourselves not what so and so said about the market but
how people are faring in our country. Are they prosperous or
in difficulty? That's how I endeavor to approach the subject.
And I hope, in the ongoing debate on trade in this country,
that we can have the maximum amount of light and the
minimum amount of heat.

Finally, I am surprised that more Americans aren't concerned about international trade policy, for it has the most
direct impact on their lives and will have an impact on their
children and grandchildren. However, Americans are a prag-
matic people. They believe in ascertaining and acting on the

facts. Therefore, I believe that in the next few years they *will* come to a decision as to how the country should proceed with respect to international trade.